They Came from Mars and Landed Outside the Farndale Avenue Church Hall in Time for the Townswomen's Guild's Coffee Morning

A Comedy

David McGillivray and
Walter Zerlin Jnr

Samuel French – London
New York – Sydney – Toronto – Hollywood

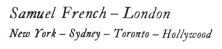 

ISBN 0 573 01665 8

Please see page iv for further copyright information.

MADE AND PRINTED IN GREAT BRITAIN BY
LATIMER TREND & COMPANY LTD PLYMOUTH
MADE IN ENGLAND

THEY CAME FROM MARS
AND LANDED OUTSIDE
THE FARNDALE AVENUE CHURCH HALL
IN TIME FOR THE
TOWNSWOMEN'S GUILD'S COFFEE MORNING

First produced at the MacRobert Arts Centre, Stirling, on 8th August, 1986, with the following cast of characters:

Mrs Reece (playing **Professor Einstein**)	Jennifer Lautrec
Thelma (playing **Jimmy** and **Susan Allsopp**)	Cindy Lee Wright
Gordon (playing **Reverend Allsopp**)	Jon Trevor
Felicity (playing **Mrs Allsopp** and **Indesit the Martian**)	Janet Sate
Norah (playing **Mrs Tompkins** and **Roberta the Robot**)	Dawn Toms

Directed by David McGillivray

CHARACTERS

Mrs Reece: elegant, bossy, enterprising; 50s.
Thelma: quick-tempered prima donna; late 40s.
Gordon: long-suffering stage manager, frozen-faced and monotonous when acting; age immaterial.
Felicity: nervous, well-meaning but incompetent actress, late 20s.
Norah: cheerful, capable, latterly semi-conscious; not young.

SYNOPSIS OF SCENES

Other Farndale Avenue comedies by
David McGillivray and Walter Zerlin Jnr
published by Samuel French

The Farndale Avenue Housing Estate Townswomen's Guild Dramatic Society's
Production of *A Christmas Carol*

The Farndale Avenue Housing Estate Townswomen's Guild Dramatic Society
Murder Mystery

The Farndale Avenue Housing Estate Townswomen's Guild Dramatic Society's
Production of *Macbeth*

The Farndale Avenue Housing Estate Townswomen's Guild Operatic Society's
Production of *The Mikado*

The Haunted Through Lounge and Recessed Dining Nook at Farndale Castle

We Found Love and an Exquisite Set of Porcelain Figurines Aboard the
SS Farndale Avenue

PROLOGUE

Music with astronomical associations ("Blue Moon", "Catch a Falling Star", "Fly Me to the Moon", etc.) plays. The stage is empty. When most of the audience are seated, Mrs Reece, elegant middle-aged Chairman of the Dramatic Society, bustles in with programmes. She is more anxious than usual. Music fades

Mrs Reece I'm terribly sorry about the delay, everyone. The Slimmers' Club were in here before us and, when I asked them to withdraw, they started throwing their weight about. Not a pretty sight. Anyway it's put us dreadfully behind and that's why we still haven't got our scenery up. Oh, hello! I'm so glad you could come. This is one of the authors, ladies and gentlemen. We've had so much fun with your piece. I hope you don't think we've taken too many liberties. The only reason we changed the setting from a nuclear power station to the vicarage is that we had the scenery left over from the Agatha Christie. Waste not, want not. And talking of scenery, everyone, we're going to have to put our stuff on the stage now so—please—no staring. Or there's always that remote possibility that someone might make a mistake. Those of you who have nothing to do can go and give your names to Mrs Wolstenholme, who's organizing a petition to make purple rinses available on the National Health. And if anyone wants reading material I've got bags of programmes here. Sorry about the creased ones. I caught my grand-daughter's guinea pig trying to make a nest out of them. (*Calling*) You can bring the things on now, ladies. But remember: fairy footsteps. We don't want to know you're there.

Mrs Reece continues selling programmes and does not look at the stage again. Music. Holding a curtain on a rod (curtain A), which hides them from the view of the audience, Gordon and Thelma enter L, carrying a table, which they deposit C before exiting R. Gordon and Thelma enter R with curtain A concealing Norah, who is carrying an ironing board and curtain B. The ironing board is placed upside-down on the table. Norah exits R behind curtain B. Gordon and Thelma exit L behind curtain A, then immediately enter and take the ironing board off R. Simultaneously Felicity, holding a vacuum cleaner, enters L behind curtain C, and Gordon and Thelma enter R behind curtain A. Felicity deposits the vacuum cleaner C and exits R. Gordon and Thelma take the table off L, then immediately enter behind curtain A and take the vacuum cleaner off R. Gordon and Thelma enter R with curtain A concealing Norah with the ironing board. Holding curtain A, Gordon and Thelma exit L, leaving Norah doing the ironing. Simultaneously Felicity, holding curtain C, enters R, and Gordon, holding curtain B, enters L. Felicity and Gordon meet C below the ironing board. Simultaneously Felicity begins to exit R and Gordon begins to exit L. Realizing that Norah is still on stage, Felicity and Gordon re-join their curtains C, then exit R with Norah and the ironing board. Holding curtain B, Gordon enters R with Felicity holding a hardboard shark. They move to C. Holding curtain D, Thelma enters L with a bucket, which she places below curtain B. Holding curtain C, Norah enters R with a plastic sack marked "Gordon's make-up", which she places below curtain D. Almost immediately Gordon and Norah exit L and Thelma exits R, revealing Felicity holding the shark. Mrs Reece sees her. Music stops

·Which scene is that in, dear?
Felicity Which scene is what in?
Mrs Reece Take it off.
Felicity We've just brought it on.
Mrs Reece Get rid of it, dear. Quickly.

Felicity clears the stage while Mrs Reece is talking to the audience

You see? This is what comes of staring at her. Please! Read your programmes. Do not look at the stage. Or there's no knowing what'll come on next. That lady there! Eyes down! If we end up with Birnam Wood I'll hold you personally responsible. Of course some of us can remember when theatres had curtains, can't we? It's not like the old days, is it? I mean this is very nice, but you wouldn't want to come here for a night out, would you? Anyone else want a programme? No? Well, I think we'll start the play then. Now, as you can see, our set is rather elaborate this year, and we have Mr Cheshire to thank for constructing the swimming pool. It looks magnificent, doesn't it? But all it consists of is six dozen bin-liners held together with Evostik. And we fill it by attaching Mr Cheshire's garden hose to one of the taps in the gentlemen's . . . (*She looks behind her, does a double-take and surveys the empty stage in disbelief*) Felicity!
Norah (*off*) Felicity!
Felicity (*off*) What?
Norah (*off*) Mrs Reece wants you.
Felicity (*off*) Now what?
Mrs Reece Quickly as you can, dear.
Felicity (*off*) I'm trying to get changed.

Felicity appears

What's wrong?
Mrs Reece It's a minor point. As you may know we're doing a play here tonight and, at first glance at any rate, there would appear to be nothing on the stage.
Felicity (*mystified*) Yes.
Mrs Reece Felicity, we're starting in thirty seconds. Bring everything in the wings on to the stage.
Felicity You told me to take it off!

Mrs Reece (*to the audience*) It's her first time on props. (*To Felicity*) One of the authors is here tonight. You're showing us all up. Now will you bring everything out here this minute?

Felicity Everything?

Mrs Reece (*to the audience*) We won't be much longer. (*To Felicity*) Yes, everything! (*To the audience*) And I'm sure we're all going to have a lovely evening. Thank you.

Mrs Reece exits

Music

Felicity turns wearily into the wings and returns carrying something which she sets on stage. She repeats this action until she has filled the stage, not only with items we have already seen, but also all manner of domestic items, theatrical paraphernalia and general junk, the more incongruous the better. The collection must include a table or desk with a drawer, three chairs and a picture

When there is barely room to move, Felicity exits

Music and House Lights fade

ACT I

The Vicarage in Farndale Avenue

The Lights come up on what is supposed to be the drawing-room of the Farndale Avenue Vicarage

Standing bemused amidst the bric-à-brac is the housekeeper Mrs Tompkins, played by the cheerful and resourceful Norah

There is the sound effect of a vacuum cleaner. Mrs Tompkins searches everywhere for the real thing, but can't find it. As a last resort she begins doing the ironing. Sound effect of the telephone ringing. Mrs Tompkins can't find that either. In desperation Mrs Tompkins picks up the iron and holds it to her ear

Mrs Tompkins Hello? Yes, this is the vicarage, but the Reverend Allsopp ain't available at present because he's over at the church hall, where the Townswomen's Guild's having their coffee morning. I'm Mrs Tompkins, the housekeeper's vicar these past twenty years. Can I be of any assistance? Cor, bless you, sir, of course I know the professor. He's the lodger's vicar—vicar's lodger, but I can't disturb him at the moment because he's in the laboratory mixing up a top-secret formula. What's that? Yes, I can give him a message. Hold on while I get the notepad. (*She looks in vain for the prop and finally picks up a portrait of "The Laughing Cavalier", which she puts on the ironing board*) Here we are, sir. Now where did I put that pencil?

A hand from offstage passes her a broom. She attempts to manipulate this

Sorry about that, sir. It was behind my ear all the time. Can I have your name? Lawks! Begging your pardon, sir, but is that *the* Jack Braithwaite, star reporter on the *Guildford Bugle*? Gulp! This is an honour and no mistake. You'll be wanting an interview with the professor, I expect? Very good, sir. What time shall I say you'll call? In an hour. Well, that'll be at—hold on a tic, sir. I'll just have a peek out of the french windows at the old church clock. (*She looks round somewhat hopelessly for the aforementioned flats*) We seem to have mislaid the french windows just at the moment. And I think the old church clock's done a bunk and all. Still, you pop round whenever you can, sir, and I'll put the kettle on. If I can find it. Bye-bye. Well, I'll just arrange these flowers and then I'll take a dip in the pool.

We hear someone blowing into a microphone in an attempt to suggest the sound of a flying saucer landing. The effect becomes wheezier

Where's that earsplitting noise coming from?

Voice (*off, gasping*) Ooh! Ran out of breath.
Mrs Tompkins It sounds like something's landing in the garden.
Voice (*off*) I can't do this tomorrow, Gordon. Not with my asthma.
Mrs Tompkins Joyce, they can hear you.
Voice (*off*) What's the next cue, love?
Gordon (*off*) Doorbell.
Mrs Tompkins Joyce!
Voice (*off*) Oh, that's on the next page. Hand us that birthday cake. I'll do the icing.
Mrs Tompkins No, just put the jam in the sponge. I'll ice it later.
Voice (*off*) Come again, love?
Mrs Tompkins I said just put the ... (*she places hand to mouth as she realizes*) ... turn the microphone off, Joyce.
Voice (*off*) Right you are.

Click

Mrs Tompkins Cripes! There's ... and don't bother with the icing ... Cripes! There's something coming down all right and it ain't Mary Poppins neither. Ah! What's that blinding light?

An inoperative electric torch is pushed through the drapes upstage

Gordon (*off*) Hang on.
Mrs Tompkins It's hurting my eyes. I can't look.
Gordon (*off*) Torch won't work.

Pause

Mrs Tompkins Shall I say "The sun must be exploding"?
Gordon (*off*) In a minute.
Mrs Reece (*off*) Use these.
Gordon (*off*) Is that all there is?
Mrs Reece (*off*) Hurry up! They're waiting.

Gordon's hands appear through the drapes and strike a match. Mrs Tompkins is looking elsewhere

Gordon (*off*) Psst!

Mrs Tompkins sees the match flame and shields her eyes

Mrs Tompkins Cor, strike a light! The sun's exploding.
Mrs Reece (*off*) Now blow it out before the Fire Officer sees it.

Gordon does so and withdraws

Mrs Tompkins Lummy, I must have had one over the eight.

Sound of a vacuum cleaner

Strewth! There's the doorbell. (*She climbs over the junk to get* L)

Felicity, a nervous, incompetent young housewife, enters as Indesit, a Martian, in a ludicrous costume that includes what is obviously a tarted-up motorcycle helmet

If you want the coffee morning, miss, it's over at the church hall.

Indesit (*gruffly*) I am a Martian. I come from Mars.

Mrs Tompkins Ooh, that's a fair old way, ain't it? Still, I told them the word would get round if they went over to Gold Blend.

Indesit You are woman who cleans?

Mrs Tompkins Yes, three mornings a week.

Indesit So my spies were correct. You will come with me.

Mrs Tompkins Where to, miss?

Indesit In my spaceship to Mars.

Mrs Tompkins Chance'd be a fine thing, young lady. As soon as I've run round with the Hoover, I've got to unblock the sink and rinse through a couple of cassocks.

Indesit This is unim——(*she coughs*) I don't think I'll bother with that voice, Norah. It hurts my throat. This is unimportant. Follow me to spaceship and bring macramé patterns.

Mrs Tompkins But I ain't got none.

Indesit You make macramé without patterns?

Mrs Tompkins Lord love-a-duck, no. I don't make macramé at all. It's a skilled art.

Indesit There must be some mistake.

Mrs Tompkins You want the Townswomen's Guild. Like I said, they're over at the church hall. They'll whistle you up a macramé owl as soon as look at you.

Indesit Enough! I must radio for further instructions. (*She brings out a walkie-talkie and pulls out the aerial, which comes off completely*) Calling all Martians. There has been administrative error. Earthwoman cannot do macramé. I understand. Over and roger. (*To Mrs Tompkins*) You are to be . . . er . . .

Mrs Tompkins Neutralized.

Indesit That's right.

Mrs Tompkins Oh, no.

Indesit cannot get her ray-gun out of its holster

(*Improvising*) Anything but that. Neutralized! That's the last thing I want to be. You're not going to neutralize me with that gun, are you?

Indesit You are to be neutralized.

Mrs Tompkins That's awful. What a thing to happen. There's too much jam on that sponge, Joyce. It'll come out the sides. Scrape some off.

While Mrs Tompkins is talking into the wings, Indesit frees the gun and points it at her

That's better. Put the top on. Press it down lightly.

Indesit (*sotto voce; to Mrs Tompkins*) Freeze.

Mrs Tompkins What?

Indesit Freeze!

Mrs Tompkins No, what does she want to freeze it for? We're having it after the interval. Oh, I see what you mean. (*She freezes*)

Indesit exits. Gordon, an awkward, stone-faced stage manager in an ill-fitting suit enters as the Reverend Allsopp and reacts to the chaotic set

Reverend Allsopp Morning, Mrs T. And what a grand morning it is to be sure. Ha-ha-ha-ha. Those ladies over at the church hall certainly are a cheerful lot. Do you know what one of them said to me? "No sugar for me, thanks, Reverend. I'm sweet enough as it is." Ha-ha-ha-ha. That gave me a good laugh. Now where did I put the notes for my sermon? I thought I left them on the bureau. (*Into the wings*) I can't find anything. I say! Mrs Reece!

Mrs Reece (*off*) Get on with the play, Gordon.

Reverend Allsopp Can't find my notes.

Mrs Reece (*off*) Bureau!

Reverend Allsopp Yes, but look.

Mrs Reece screams off

Mrs Reece (*off*) Who made that mess on the stage?

Reverend Allsopp It wasn't me. It was Felicity.

Mrs Reece (*off*) You're supposed to be the stage manager, Gordon.

Reverend Allsopp I was doing my make-up.

Mrs Reece (*off*) And one of the authors is in tonight! How embarrassing.

Reverend Allsopp I've got to have my notes, Mrs Reece.

Making tiny movements with her eyes and head, Mrs Tompkins tries to draw Allsopp's attention to where the notes are semi-hidden

Mrs Reece (*off*) Just say: "It's all right. I've found them."

Reverend Allsopp It's all right. Mrs Reece has found them.

He continues looking for them while Mrs Tompkins continues, with bigger movements, to show him where they are

Ah, yes. Tell me, Mrs T, how does this sound to you? He reads from notes. "As I looked up at the sky last night I was reminded of ... something about it really big ... and ... something else I can't remember." Well, Mrs T? Give me your honest opinion. Mrs T, Mrs T, what's the matter, what's the matter? Good gracious, she seems to be in a catatonic stupor. (*He still hasn't approached, nor even looked at, the manically twitching Mrs Tompkins*)

Nor does he look at Felicity, who enters as Mrs Allsopp, the vicar's wife. She is still wearing Indesit's space helmet

Mrs Allsopp Ah, hello, darling. I thought I heard you come back. I've just been potting some geraniums.

Reverend Allsopp Where'd you put my notes?

Mrs Allsopp Herbert, you're as white as a sheet. Is anything wrong?

Reverend Allsopp Yes, you haven't set my notes.

In desperation Mrs Tompkins climbs over furniture in order to reach the notes, which she thrusts into Reverend Allsopp's hands

Oh, thanks.

Mrs Allsopp What's the matter with Mrs T?

During the following, Mrs Tompkins climbs back to her position

Reverend Allsopp She's completely lifeless.

Mrs Allsopp Let me see. (*She climbs over the furniture to reach Mrs Tompkins*)

Reverend Allsopp (*noticing the superfluous helmet*) You've still got your helmet on.

Mrs Allsopp I know. I can't get it off. Just forget about it. Mrs T, Mrs T!

Reverend Allsopp It's no good. I've tried everything.

Mrs Allsopp Have you tried everything?

Reverend Allsopp Yes. It's no good.

Mrs Allsopp And nothing did any good?

Reverend Allsopp No. And I've tried everything.

Mrs Allsopp We must do something.

Mrs Tompkins (*prompting*) The line about the professor.

Mrs Allsopp The line about the professor.

Reverend Allsopp Maybe our lodger, the professor, will know what to do.

Mrs Allsopp There's no time for that, darling. Maybe our lodger, the professor, will know what to do.

Reverend Allsopp You stay here. I'll go.

Mrs Allsopp No, I want to stay here with poor Mrs T. Will you go?

Reverend Allsopp There's no time for that. I'll get the professor.

Mrs Allsopp I'll tell the children to stay in their rooms. They mustn't see this.

Thelma, middle-aged, bad-tempered prima donna, enters as the Allsopps' eight-year-old son Jimmy. During the ensuing dialogue Mrs Tompkins resumes chattering into the wings

Jimmy Morning, Mum. Did I hear Dad telling our lodger, the professor, that something terrible had happened?

Mrs Allsopp Of course not, Jimmy. You must have been dreaming.

Reverend Allsopp Professor! Come up here quickly. Something terrible's happened.

Jimmy Oh, flip and blow.

Reverend Allsopp Language, my boy.

He and Jimmy are facing each other in a confined space

Jimmy Sorry, Dad. Didn't see you there. It's just that it's so boring here at the vicarage for an eight-year-old like me. I want a bit of excitement.

Mrs Allsopp Jimmy, put your school uniform back on this minute. You can't go swimming now.

Jimmy Oh, please, Mum. I'm boiling.

Mrs Allsopp Come and give your mother a big kiss and a hug, Jimmy. There's something I want you to do.

Jimmy Right-o, Mum.

He and Mrs Allsopp climb towards each other

Who's responsible for this?

Reverend Allsopp Don't look at me.

Mother and son embrace, Jimmy towering over the petite Mrs Allsopp

Mrs Allsopp My, you are getting a big boy, Jimmy.

Reverend Allsopp You'll soon be as tall as your mother, young lad.

Jimmy Mum, Dad: when I grow up, shall I be able to go to whist drives like you?

Mrs Allsopp Of course you shall, you little tinker. But right now I want you to take your crayons into the garden and design me a few loose covers for the patio suite.

Jimmy I will if you'll tell me something.

Mrs Allsopp What's that, you young scamp?

Jimmy Why is Mrs T standing there as stiff and frozen as a statue?

Everyone waits for Mrs Tompkins to finish her highly animated conversation. Eventually she realizes and freezes again

Mrs Allsopp What are we going to tell him, Benjie?

Reverend Allsopp He'll have to be told the truth, Marlene.

Mrs Allsopp Of course. Jimmy something terrible has happened.

Jimmy Wow! I must tell my beautiful elder sister, Susan, who's playing her cello in the conservatory. (*He begins climbing off* R)

Mrs Allsopp Stop him, darling. He's making for the door.

Reverend Allsopp Ah, just missed him. He ran out between my legs.

Jimmy is stranded on top of something

Jimmy This is preposterous.

Mrs Allsopp I'll sort it out in the interval, Thelma.

Mrs Reece enters as the bald-headed Professor Einstein. She is in a white coat and carries a test tube

Einstein Not so fast, you young whippersnapper. Where'd you think you're off to, eh?

Mrs Allsopp Professor, thank goodness you're here.

Einstein Sorry I've been such a long time, but I've been putting the last few ingredients in this top-secret formula.

Reverend Allsopp Is this the new explosive you were telling me about, Prof?

Einstein Yes, it's so powerful that one drop is enough to destroy the universe. (*He drops the test tube*) Never mind. I'll wipe it up later. Now what's all this I hear about something terrible happening?

Mrs Allsopp It's Mrs T, Professor. Look!

Einstein climbs towards Mrs Tompkins

Einstein Easier said than done, isn't it?

Reverend Allsopp Why are you shining that light into her eyes, Prof?

Einstein Hang on a jiff, Gordon. Who do you think I am? Edmund Hilary?

Jimmy I've had enough of this, Phoebe. This perpetual embarrassment. I'm resigning as Social Secretary.

Einstein Do try to stay in character, Thelma. We're supposed to be men. Oh, would you believe it? I've broken my best nail.

Reverend Allsopp Why are you shining that light into her eyes, Prof?

Einstein Oh, dear, he won't be happy till he gets an answer, will he? (*He brings out a torch pen, hurries the last few steps, trips and jabs the torch pen into Mrs Tompkins' eye*)

Mrs Tompkins Ow!

Einstein Sorry, dear. Was that your eye?

Mrs Allsopp Take your hand away. Let me see.

Einstein (*to the audience*) I don't think it's anything serious.

Reverend Allsopp Why are you shining——?

Einstein Oh, all right, Gordon! For heaven's sake.

Mrs Tompkins is flailing about, threshing her arms

I'm just ascertaining that Mrs T is in suspended animation, unable to move a muscle.

Mrs Allsopp We need some Optrex or something.

Einstein (*into the wings*) Have you got an eyebath, Joyce? An eyebath, dear. There's too much water in that icing sugar.

Mrs Tompkins I said I'd do the icing!

Einstein Norah's doing the icing, dear. You concentrate on the sound cues.

Mrs Allsopp I think you missed the eyeball.

Einstein Oh, what a blessing. Although if I had poked it out you'd have been perfect casting for *Oedipus Rex*. But I mustn't be flippant.

Jimmy Gosh, Professor Einstein, what do you think happened to Mrs T to make her like that?

Einstein Don't be alarmed, everyone, but I think she's in the thrall of an extra-testicle hypnosis.

Jimmy What does that mean?

Einstein I'll explain, Jimmy. Come and sit on my lap.

A chair is found. Einstein sits. Jimmy sits on his lap and bounces up and down

No, no, no! Get up, Thelma. We agreed no bouncing.

Einstein sits on Jimmy's lap

You see, Jimmy, I have reason to believe we're not alone in the universe.

Jimmy Have the Martians landed?

Einstein You're a bright boy, Jimmy. What do you want to be when you grow up?

Mrs Allsopp screams

Jimmy It's not your turn.

Mrs Allsopp Sorry.

Jimmy I'd like to be a scientist like you, Professor Einstein. (*To Mrs Allsopp*) Thank you.

Mrs Allsopp screams

Reverend Allsopp Cicely, what is it?

Mrs Allsopp There's a flying saucer in the garden.

Einstein This could be our opportunity to communicate with alien beings.

Jimmy Can you see anything through these binoculars, Professor?

Einstein gives up hunting for the binoculars and mimes them

Einstein Yes, it's Martians all right, and it looks like they mean business.

Mrs Allsopp But why would they want to be so horrid to Mrs T?

Einstein It's a mystery to me, Mrs Allsopp. But we can at least return the dear old soul to normality.

Reverend Allsopp How?

Einstein I've developed some re-animating capsules. Would you pass them to me, Jimmy? They're on the mantelpiece.

Jimmy I don't think I'll be able to reach, Professor.

Einstein (*to Mrs Allsopp*) Have you come across the fireplace in your travels, dear?

Mrs Allsopp Fireplace ...

Einstein Yes. It had a fire in it, as I recall.

Reverend Allsopp I put it in the swimming pool.

Jimmy Oh, that'll do the capsules a lot of good.

Reverend Allsopp The capsules are here somewhere. In a handbag.

Mrs Allsopp (*without the others hearing*) I know where that is.

Mrs Allsopp exits

Einstein and Reverend Allsopp hunt for the handbag while Jimmy stands watching disdainfully

Einstein A handbag? (*To Mrs Tompkins*) Can you see a handbag?

Mrs Tompkins I can't see anything!

Einstein Silly of me. Well, don't you worry, Mrs T, because we'll find these capsules in an absolute trice and then you'll be back on your knees, scraping out the inside of the oven like the little trojan you are.

Reverend Allsopp has found a wind-up toy and is playing with this instead

It's a jolly good thing I invented those capsules, isn't it? But I thought they'd come in handy when I picked up these radio signals from Mars. They came through just after *A Book at Bedtime*. You can imagine my surprise. What's this? (*Finding the handbag*) Bingo! It's all right, Reverend ... Reverend!

Reverend Allsopp puts down the toy

We'll just give Mrs T a couple of dozen of these. They'll stimulate her electrical impulses, counteract the alien hypnogenesis, and clear up her sinuses.

Reverend Allsopp She's looking better already, Prof.

Einstein Yes, the colour's coming back to her cheeks, isn't it? Now come on, Jimmy, let's you and me keep an eye on these invaders from outer space.

Mrs Allsopp enters with jar of capsules

Mrs Allsopp Found them.

Einstein We've done it, dear. We're on the next page now.

Mrs Allsopp What did you give her?

Einstein The capsules, dear! They were in that handbag.

Mrs Allsopp goes to the handbag and examines the capsule jar inside with horror

Do you see what I see, Jimmy? The Martians are bringing all the Townswomen out of the church hall. It looks like they're examining them. Who's that they've got there, Mrs Allsopp? Is that Flossie, the dental nurse?

Mrs Allsopp How many of these did you give her?

Einstein Oh, she's such a worry-wart. I don't know. A handful. Why?

Mrs Allsopp They're my Valium.

Reverend Allsopp How are you feeling now, Mrs T?

Mrs Tompkins Very ... nice.

Reverend Allsopp Well, you've been in the wars, haven't you, old stick? Can you describe the blackguard responsible?

Mrs Tompkins Your trousers are too short, Gordon.

Reverend Allsopp Looks like she can't remember a thing.

Jimmy What else is new?

Einstein Can you keep an eye on her, Reverend? Jimmy and I are just monitoring these tricky little Martian devils.

Mrs Allsopp tries to clamber towards Mrs Tompkins, but she is already climbing somewhere else

Jimmy They seem to be looking for one particular lady, Professor Einstein. Do you think they're going to take her back to Mars?

Reverend Allsopp I hope not. I have few enough parishioners as it is.

Einstein This is a job for the police. I'm phoning them right away. (*He looks around*) Mrs Allsopp! Can you oblige, dear?

Mrs Tompkins hands him the iron

What do I want this for?

Mrs Tompkins Hot line.

Einstein Thank you, dear. Hello, hello. As I feared, the line's been cut.

Mrs Allsopp Oh, no. What are we going to do?

Einstein Someone will have to climb unobserved through the tiny basement window, swim across the marsh, and semaphore to the police from the top of the electricity pylon.

Mrs Tompkins Oh, I'll do that.

Jimmy You won't!

Mrs Tompkins Yes, I can pick up the shopping on the way back.

Einstein Don't you trouble yourself, dear.

Mrs Tompkins I'm kidding! Cor blimey, you wouldn't catch me doing anything so stupid. (*To a member of the audience*) Oh, hello, darling! Haven't seen you for ages ...

Jimmy Will somebody shut her up?

Mrs Allsopp Come and sit down, Mrs T.

She prevents Mrs Tompkins from toppling off the edge of the stage by pulling her into a chair

Reverend Allsopp But none of us is small enough to squeeze through that tiny basement window.

Jimmy I am, Dad.

Reverend Allsopp No, Jimmy. It's out of the question because it's much too dangerous.

Jimmy Oh, please, Dad. Let me try.

Reverend Allsopp All right.

Jimmy Super! This is my chance to help mankind like my hero Professor Einstein. Now where did I put my junior semaphore kit?

Jimmy exits

Mrs Tompkins (*to the audience*) He gets killed.

Einstein Norah!

Mrs Allsopp gags Mrs Tompkins with her own duster

Reverend Allsopp There goes our brave son scampering away like a young buck. Go on, Jimmy. You can do it. Hoo——

Pause

Einstein ⎤
Mrs Allsopp ⎦ (*together*) Hooray!

Reverend Allsopp —ray.

Mrs Allsopp He heard us. Look! He's waving.

Einstein Ssshh everybody! That Martian patrolman heard us as well. Oh, spit! He's seen the young'un.

Reverend Allsopp Duck, Jimmy. He's got a ray-gun.

Einstein Too late.

Mrs Allsopp Is he—is he . . . ?

Reverend Allsopp Yes. He's been neutralized. How perfectly ghastly.

Mrs Allsopp cries

Jimmy enters with semaphore flags

Jimmy Well, I'm off now. Wish me luck, everyone.

Jimmy goes out, whistling "Colonel Bogey"

Mrs Allsopp He was so young.

Mrs Tompkins Young? Her?

Mrs Allsopp What shall we tell our beautiful daughter Susan?

Sound of a vacuum cleaner

There's someone at the door.

Reverend Allsopp It's a young man in a trilbycoat with a trench card in his press.

Einstein It sounds like Jack Braithwaite, star reporter on the *Guildford Bugle*.

Mrs Tompkins That's it! (*Singing*) "It's the boogie-woogie bugle boy from company B!"

Einstein (*pointedly*) Why don't we invite the young man in, Reverend?

Reverend Allsopp Come in, young man.

Very, very long pause

At long last Thelma, glowering, enters in a dressing-gown

Thelma Got any kaolin and morphine?

Einstein What's wrong? Where's Hilda?

Thelma She's in the loo.

Einstein (*to the audience*) Pardon me.

Einstein and Thelma exit

Reverend and Mrs Allsopp wait, embarrassed and bewildered

Mrs Tompkins (*imitating Einstein*) Pardon me.

Pause

(*Snootily*) Pardon *me*!

Pause

(*Singing*) "Pardon me, boy. Is that the Chattanooga choo-choo?
Track twenty-nine,
I can't remember the line.
I can afford . . ."

Mrs Tompkins continues the song as she leaves the stage and exits via the auditorium

Reverend and Mrs Allsopp watch her departure with horror. Another long, agonized pause. Reverend Allsopp begins absentmindedly ironing his notes, but stops when Mrs Allsopp glares at him. Reverend Allsopp studies Mrs Allsopp's helmet. She notices him. Several times he indicates the helmet and a nearby table or desk with a drawer. She doesn't understand. Reverend Allsopp opens the drawer and puts Mrs Allsopp's head inside it. With the drawer acting as a makeshift vice, Reverend Allsopp attempts to extricate Mrs Allsopp's head from the helmet. Bent over Mrs Allsopp's semi-procumbent form, the Reverend Allsopp makes heaving movements that look extremely ambiguous

Einstein enters

Einstein (*to the audience*) I'm sorry about this, ladies and . . . (*He sees the Reverend and Mrs Allsopp and stares at them in astonishment*) What *are* you doing?

Reverend Allsopp stops dead

Reverend Allsopp Nothing.

Einstein (*to the audience*) As you'll have gathered, Hilda Bristow, who's playing Jack Braithwaite, has been taken poorly. I'm afraid she's got the tro——the ru——a gyppy ... she's got an upset stomach ...

Reverend Allsopp surreptitiously returns to grappling with Mrs Allsopp

And I don't think she's going to be joining us for a while.

He looks at Reverend Allsopp and waits for him to stop, which he does

But we are going to go on as best we can. And I want you to pay particular attention to this: the leading man won't be physically present. I hope that won't bother you too much.

Once again he notices Reverend Allsopp's fumbling

Oh, what are you two playing at?

Mrs Allsopp I can't get my head out of the desk, Mrs Reece.

Einstein As if I haven't got enough to worry about. One of the authors is in tonight. This is too bad. (*He frees Mrs Allsopp*)

Meanwhile Mrs Tompkins enters the auditorium

There. Now let that be——

He slams the Reverend Allsopp's fingers in the drawer. He cries out and leaps about

I don't believe this. (*He comes down* C) Please accept my apologies. We're making an absolute pig's ear of your delightful piece. Where are you?

Mrs Tompkins Oh, the author's gone home, Phoebe.

Einstein He's what?

Mrs Tompkins He's gone home. He said he thought the housekeeper was very good.

Einstein Norah? Get back on this stage at once. The very idea.

Mrs Tompkins returns to the stage

Mrs Allsopp Has the author gone home?

Einstein Will you address yourself to the matter in hand, Felicity? Now let's get on with the play. Come in!

Pause. Then Einstein mimes shaking hands with someone

Well ... this is very unexpected.

Reverend Allsopp Whatever you want, young man, I'm afraid I can't see you right now.

Einstein As I suspected, Reverend, this is Jack Braithwaite, a gentleman of the press. Won't you sit down, Jack?

Einstein, Reverend and Mrs Allsopp all bring up chairs. Mrs Tompkins sits on Einstein's

So you want to interview me about my experiments, do you? (*To Mrs Tompkins*) What are you doing?

Mrs Tompkins I've got to sit down.

Einstein Well, not there. Jack's sitting there, isn't he?

Mrs Allsopp No, he's not. He's here.

Reverend Allsopp I thought he was here.

Einstein My! Isn't he a will-o'-the-wisp? (*To Mrs Tompkins*) Deep breaths, dear.

Mrs Tompkins begins passing into unconsciousness. Einstein periodically pushes her upright

Reverend Allsopp You'll have to forgive my housekeeper, Mr Braithwaite, but she's just been neutered.

Mrs Allsopp That's why the house is in such a state.

Einstein You're speechless, aren't you, Jack? Let me try and explain. As you drove up to the vicarage you may have noticed some strange-looking creatures in our toolshed. You're not going to believe this, but they're Martians.

Reverend Allsopp Yes, we're in a tight spot all right unless *pause* snaps fingers why yes that's it: why don't we escape in Mr Braithwaite's car?

Mrs Allsopp Would that be all right, Mr Braithwaite?

Einstein Just say if it isn't. (*Pause*) Well, that's settled then.

Mrs Allsopp I'll go and get our beautiful daughter, Susan, and we'll select something light and casual for the journey.

Mrs Allsopp exits

Reverend Allsopp Great Scott! Look what the Martians are doing to Jack's car.

Sound of a vacuum cleaner

Einstein Yes, they're cleaning it. Isn't that thoughtful? (*Into the wings*) Joyce, will you put that cake down and run the tape on? (*To the audience*) Sorry. But now the Martians are destroying Jack's car. (*Into the wings*) Go!

Sound of a vacuum cleaner

(*Despairingly*) With the Hoover.

Reverend Allsopp This is terrible.

Einstein I know. And the icing's too runny as well.

Thelma enters as Susan. She is in a bathing costume and bathing hat and has a towel round her shoulders

Susan Daddy, what on earth's going on? I'm absolutely exhausted after my cello practice, and I was going to swim half a dozen lengths of the pool. But Mummy says we've got to zoom off to the police station, and where, oh, where is my mischievous brother, Jimmy? Oh, sorry. I didn't know you had company.

Only Einstein notices Mrs Tompkins sliding off the chair

Reverend Allsopp Susan, this is Jack Braithwaite from the *Guildford Bugle*.

Susan Golly, Mr Braithwaite, you're hardly seeing me at my best.

Einstein And vice versa.
Reverend Allsopp Come and give Daddy a great big hug.
Einstein And bring Mrs T with you.

Susan reluctantly takes hold of Mrs Tompkins and pulls her to her feet

Susan Wake up, Norah!
Mrs Tompkins Not tonight, Victor. It's only Wednesday.

Susan drags her to the table

Susan This is no fun, you know, Norah.
Mrs Tompkins It never has been, Victor.

Norah is seated on the table and held in position by Susan

Susan It's not bad news, is it, Daddy?
Reverend Allsopp Look at you, Susan—an Olympic swimming champion.
Susan Just off to give my first concert at Carnegie Hall.
Reverend Allsopp And it seems like only yesterday I was dandling you on my knee.
Susan Do you remember the time that hedgehog nibbled my garibaldi when we were picnicking in the sun-kissed Dingly Dell?
Reverend Allsopp And that frosty Christmas Eve when we invited the carol singers in for mulled wine and roast chestnuts?
Susan Yes. It's funny how both those occasions remind me of dear little Jimmy's face lighting up with laughter.
Reverend Allsopp He was a fine, fine boy.
Susan Daddy, why are you speaking in the past tense?
Reverend Allsopp I can't keep it from you any longer, my dear.
Susan It's not bad news, is it, Daddy?
Reverend Allsopp Look at you, Susan—an Olympic cello champion.
Susan Just off to swim round Carnegie Hall.
Reverend Allsopp And it seems like only yesterday you were dandling me on your knee.
Susan Do you remember the time that carol singer nibbled my Dingly Dell when we were picnicking in the frost?
Reverend Allsopp And that sun-kissed Christmas Eve when we invited the garibaldis in for roast hedgehog?
Susan Yes. It's funny how both those occasions remind me of dear little Jimmy's face lighting up with laughter.
Reverend Allsopp He was a fine, fine boy.
Mrs Allsopp Daddy, why are you speaking in the past tense?
Reverend Allsopp I can't keep it from you any longer, my dear.
Susan It's not bad knees, is it, Daddy?
Reverend Allsopp Look at you, Susan—an Olympic hedgehog champion.
Susan Just off for a swim in the dingly garibaldis.
Reverend Allsopp And it seems like only yesterday we were roasting little Jimmy with mulled chestnuts for a picnic in Carnegie Hall.
Susan Do you remember . . . anything?
Reverend Allsopp It's not bad news, is it, Daddy—Susan!

Susan Look at you, Daddy—dandling your dingles in the mulled wine and kissing bald carol singers' sun-kissed knees.

Reverend Allsopp It seems like only yesterday we were nibbling little Gary Carnegie's Olympic chestnuts ... in the hall. He was a fine newsboy.

Pause

Einstein I think you're over-simplifying things.

Susan (*loosening her grip on Mrs Tompkins*) My poor brother!

Einstein
Reverend Allsopp } (*together*) Don't let her go!

Susan How did it happen?

Reverend Allsopp It started in the toolshed.

Susan Who are those bizarre-looking people?

Reverend Allsopp Martians.

Susan They don't look as though they're from Guildford.

Reverend Allsopp No, they're from Mars.

Susan It's almost as if they had come from another planet.

Reverend Allsopp Mars.

Susan Daddy, they're not Martians, are they?

Einstein What makes you say that?

Susan I just know it! Ah! (*She loosens her grip on Mrs Tompkins*)

Einstein
Reverend Allsopp } (*together*) Don't let her go!

Susan (*infuriated; to Mrs Tompkins*) Will you sit up? (*She slaps Mrs Tompkins round the face*) Jack, help me to a chair. I'm coming over queer. (*She sits*)

Rallying slightly, Mrs Tompkins assumes that Reverend Allsopp has hit her. She slaps him. He staggers backwards into Einstein. Meanwhile, Mrs Tompkins meanders round the stage in the direction of Susan

Reverend Allsopp I think these two young people have fallen head over heels in love with each other.

Einstein They look as though they're in another world, don't they? Especially Jack.

Susan I'm so glad you're here, Jack.

Einstein He came to interview me about my robot.

Susan You mean Roberta the robot?

Reverend Allsopp The Super-Townswoman?

Mrs Tompkins curls up on Susan's lap and puts her arms round her shoulders

Einstein That's the girl. I've just finished programming her to help out at coffee mornings. She'll be able to whip up a chocolate torte and butter fifty sandwiches simultaneously.

Susan I bet those beastly Martians wish they had her.

Einstein By Jove! I think this young lassie's stumbled on the truth. The Martians want Roberta.

Reverend Allsopp And they're checking all the ladies in Farndale Avenue until they find her.

Susan dumps Mrs Tompkins on the floor

Einstein Quick, everybody. Down to the basement. Gordon! Can you take Norah, please? We must make sure Roberta's safely locked away.

Reverend Allsopp begins to drag Mrs Tompkins off

Mrs Tompkins (*mumbling*) Is it over? Did we win?
Reverend Allsopp Not you, Jack. You stay here with Susan.
Mrs Tompkins (*mumbling*) Not you, Jack. Who's Jack?

Mrs Tompkins and Reverend Allsopp exit

Susan (*preventing Einstein from going*) Phoebe!
Einstein Yes, dear? What is it?
Susan You don't honestly expect me to do this next scene, do you?
Einstein Of course. Why not?
Susan A love scene on my own?
Einstein You have to create the illusion, dear. Make us believe that Jack is here. You can do it. Remember Monsieur Duvivier's mime classes . . . (*He demonstrates feeling along an imaginary wall*)
Susan I've suffered enough indignities for one evening, thank you. I am not about to stand on this stage and play with myself.
Einstein Come along now, dear. This is quite simple. Jack's here as large as life. Here he is! So happy to be alone with you.
Susan Are you sure you want to get mixed up with me, Jack?
Einstein He's back here actually.
Susan Who's this then? The invisible man?
Einstein Thelma! He's here. Look! I'm holding his . . . (*he realizes that his mime of holding Jack's hand could be misconstrued and he moves his hand higher*) . . . hand. Oh, have it your own way. Jack thinks he's falling in love with you, dear.
Susan Oh, Jack! Let's treasure these few precious moments before Mars conquers the earth.
Einstein Jack won't let that happen.
Susan You can't hide the truth from me, Jack. I can see right through you. Oh! What's all that shouting in the basement?
Einstein I can't imagine. Oh, it's me.

Einstein exits, then enters, out of breath

Bad news, Jack.
Susan Roberta's escaped?
Einstein Worse than that. Roberta's escaped.
Susan How did it happen?
Einstein I've been a fool. I left her unattended in her bargain-hunting mode.
Susan Oh, no! And there's ten p off Lurpak at Tesco's.
Einstein Exactly. Even as we speak she's probably stripping the cold cabinets of every Tesco's from here to Penzance.

Reverend Allsopp enters

Reverend Allsopp I've found her.

Susan Where?

Reverend Allsopp Running towards the house and looking half-crazed.

Susan Well, who wouldn't be at the thought of those big savings on Danish butter?

Einstein It's not because of that, Susan. I've just remembered that your brother programmed Roberta's pleasure centres to be stimulated only by polyunsaturated low-fat spread. She's probably blown a diode.

Reverend Allsopp Stand back, Susan! The professor's robot is about to burst through the door in a frenzied electronic rampage.

Norah enters in a metallic costume as Roberta the robot. She staggers aimlessly

Einstein It's as I thought: she's completely uncontrollable.

Roberta collapses on top of Reverend Allsopp

Careful of her power-packed arms, Jack.

He manipulates one of Roberta's arms, which flops feebly around

One swipe could render you senseless.

He accidentally hits Reverend Allsopp with Roberta's arm

Reverend Allsopp Watch it!

Einstein Sorry, dear.

Reverend Allsopp I don't like that look in her eye, Prof. I think she's preparing to call upon hidden reserves of superstrength.

Roberta's head lolls and she begins snoring

Einstein Yes, this next surge of energy could be devastating.

He and Allsopp manage to heave Roberta upright and fold her across a piece of furniture

Reverend Allsopp Well, that was incredible.

Susan I never thought the chandelier would stand her weight.

Einstein We must get her back into the basement before the Martians capture her.

Indesit enters

Indesit I am a Martian. I come from Mars.

Einstein Aren't you going to do the funny voice, dear?

Indesit No, because it hurts my throat, Mrs——

Susan screams so loudly that the startled Indesit drops her ray-gun

Einstein Jack says, "Steady on there, Susan."

Susan I'm all right, Jack.

Indesit I will now take Super-Townswoman.

Einstein Jack says, "That's what you think, Martian."

Indesit Resistance is futile. Super-Townswoman will respond only to my superior intellgigen . . . intellingen . . . ingellintence . . .

Einstein Intelligence.
Indesit Intelligence. Thank you. Super-Townswoman! Walk towards me.

Einstein and Reverend Allsopp laboriously balance Roberta in a standing position and then try to propel her towards Indesit. It is obvious that she is not going to get very far

Roberta It's not bad news, is it, Daddy? (*She crumples to the ground*)
Indesit Now perform a triple somersault with two half-turns.
Einstein No, don't bother. The walking towards you was jolly convincing.
Indesit All right then. Farewell, earthlings.
Einstein Jack says, "Just one more thing."
Indesit I say, "What?"
Einstein "Take that, you interplanetary kidnapper."

Indesit staggers backwards as if hit

Susan Bravo, Jack! Give her one for me.

Music: "Dick Barton Theme". Indesit lurches around the stage, putting herself in a half-nelson, wristlock and other wrestling holds, while Einstein, Reverend Allsopp and Susan offer diffident support

Einstein Come on, Jack.
Reverend Allsopp Give her the old one-two.
Susan Let's show these Martians what we're made of.
Einstein Hurrah.
Reverend Allsopp Give her the old one-two.
Einstein Keep your guard up, Jack.
Susan Bob and weave.
Einstein Float like a butterfly, sting like a bee.
Reverend Allsopp Give her the old one-two.

Indesit throws herself to the ground. Music stops. Cheering

Susan Jack, you were just—out of sight.

Indesit raises herself up and aims her ray-gun

Einstein Look out behind you, Jack.

Susan screams

Reverend Allsopp Oh, no. Jack's been neutralized. What rotten luck.
Indesit Thus perish all enemas of Mars ... enemies of Mars. Well, we'd better get a move on. Do not attempt to follow us.

She tries without success to lift Roberta. She gives Einstein her ray-gun, but still has difficulty. Einstein tells Reverend Allsopp to help. Together Indesit and Reverend Allsopp begin removing Roberta

Susan Professor, that hateful Martian has taken poor Roberta into the flying saucer and closed the hatch behind them.
Indesit Have a heart, Thelma.
Susan (*firmly*) Now they're preparing for take-off.

Indesit Take her off, Gordon! I'm taking off!

Indesit exits

Roberta Gordon, you naughty boy!

Roberta and Reverend Allsopp exit

Einstein An unidentified flying object is about to depart Guildford. This could be one of the most incredible spectacles ever witnessed by man.

Rumbling is heard. Einstein and Susan tremble from the vibrations

Wearing a flying saucer round her waist and clinging on to Roberta, Indesit enters

Einstein gives her back her ray-gun

Indesit shuffles off, waving

Susan What now, Professor?

Einstein Well, I'll reanimate Jack and little Jimmy, and then I suggest a light lunch before going after the Martians and rescuing Roberta.

Reverend Allsopp enters

Reverend Allsopp Hold hard, Prof. Are you suggesting a journey into space?

Einstein That's right, Reverend. Tell your wife you may not be back for Evensong.

Susan But how on earth are we going to leave earth?

Einstein Why, Susan, in the rocket I've built in the basement.

Susan gasps, then nudges Reverend Allsopp, who gasps as well. Brief tableau

(*To the audience*) That's the end of this bit. But there's lots more coming up after the interval so go and have a cup of tea—and a Mars bar!—and we'll see you in outer space.

Black-out

Everyone exits

The House Lights come up. Music: "Mars" from The Planets Suite. *During the interval the stage is cleared and a female member of the audience is chosen to judge the Flower Arranging Competition*

ENTR'ACTE

At the end of the interval Mrs Reece mounts the stage. A spot comes up C

Mrs Reece Are we all reassembled? Anyone gone AWOL?

Felicity's head appears from the wings

Felicity The author hasn't come back, Mrs Reece.
Mrs Reece I thought you were disentangling the coat-hangers, dear.
Felicity Finished.
Mrs Reece Well then, go round the hand basins with a damp Spontex.
Felicity Tch.

Felicity withdraws

Mrs Reece Thank you, dear. Regrettably the author has had to leave due to a prior engagement. And I think it was jolly important because on the way out he said to Mrs Frobisher that if he stayed any longer he wouldn't be responsible for the consequences. Still, wasn't it nice of him to pop in? Because he's a very busy man, you know. Now just before we go on, I thought you might like to see some photos of our coach trip to London. I've got them here somewhere. Really! This bag is like a black hole. Incidentally many thanks to all those who suggested remedies for poor Hilda's tummy upset. I do agree that the old herbal cures are often the best. It was an awful chore getting the ornamental privet through the liquidizer. But it does look terribly nutritious. And we'll be giving it to her as soon as we can get her off the toilet. We're all rooting for you, Hilda, so keep your five and nine on, and we'll see you in Act Two, God willing. Where are those photos? Anyone back there got the snaps we took in London?

The spot snaps out

Oh, do look out for Norah. Look, she's fallen across the lighting board. Walk her up and down, Joyce. Keep her on the move.

Norah laughs uproariously, off

And can we have the lights on again, please?

While practically every light in the theatre is switched on and then off, Mrs Reece continues talking

I want to assure you all that Norah is as right as rain. She's a bit wobbly on her pins. But I think it's just a bad case of stage fright. So if I find out who's been calling me a drug-pusher I shall be down on them like a ton of bricks. Joyce, this isn't a disco, you know.
Voice (*off*) Are the big lights on now?
Mrs Reece No, that's the microphone, dear.

Voice (*off*) Oh, gawd.

Click

Mrs Reece It's that switch there. Underneath the baking soda.

A spot comes up c

Thank you. You haven't seen those photos, have you, Joyce? The ones of the outing. Oh, Joyce, how could you? Scrape off the sponge mixture and give them to me. (*She goes to wings and waits*) You've left a bit of egg on that one. (*She is handed small photos*) Look at that. Yolk all the way up Nelson's Column. He doesn't wear a red hat, does he? Oh, it's a glacé cherry. That's a pretty one, isn't it? Can you people at the back see all right? No? Well, it's Regent Street by night. Oh, no, it's not. It's inside the coach and the flash didn't go off. There's Thelma Greenwood inflating her appliance. She didn't know we were taking that one. Now these green ones didn't come out very well. But they're of us at the National Theatre. That's me. And that's Lord Thingumijig. And just behind him you can see Mrs Playfair. Do you remember Mrs Playfair? She's with the Bromley Light Operatic now. Or something. And here she is just about to be terribly ill. Over his Lordship. Well, not really over him. It just missed him. So that was all right. But all I can say is that, if you go and see this beautiful theatre, don't have any more than two slices of the chocolate cream gâteau. Because it's wicked. Oh! This is us in the King's Road in Chelsea. There's me talking to a Chelsea Pensioner. Actually it's Thelma in her red mac. I'm being a bit naughty. that's me being followed round Sloane Square by an eggstain. This one . . . oh, no. You can't see that one. That was nothing. Oh, this is a funny one. This'll give you a giggle. We went to one of those medieval banquets, and somebody, who shall be nameless, had a little too much mead. And before we knew what was happening she was up on the table singing, "I'm one of the ruins that Cromwell knocked about a bit." Well, fortunately Mrs Beasley whipped out her Instamatic and here——

Thelma enters

Thelma We're ready to start Act Two, Phoebe.
Mrs Reece Oh. Well, I'll show you the rest afterwards.
Thelma Not that one, you won't.
Mrs Reece It's just a bit of fun, dear.
Thelma Is it? I notice you didn't show them this one.
Mrs Reece Thelma, don't you dare!
Thelma This is Phoebe quite early in the morning . . .
Mrs Reece That's all the photos we've got time for . . .
Thelma Before she's made herself presentable . . .
Mrs Reece Yes, that's very amusing. Let's get on with Act Two, shall we? And remind me to give you the results of the Flower Arranging Competition.

Mrs Reece hustles Thelma off

The Lights fade to Black-out

ACT II

SCENE 1

Outer space

Black-out

Taped voices are heard

Einstein's voice This is your captain, Professor Einstein, speaking. Welcome aboard flight number one to Mars. Are the posigrade stabilizers pre-activated?

Reverend Allsopp's voice Yes, Prof.

Einstein's voice Is the trajectory verification system operative?

Jack's voice Yes, Professor.

Einstein's voice Is the handbrake off?

Jimmy's voice Yes, Professor.

Einstein's voice Good. Then prepare for countdown.

Jimmy's voice Gosh, Professor, this is a topping adventure. Bags I convert the thrust modulator.

Einstein's voice Wait a minute. What's Jimmy doing here?

Jimmy's voice What do you mean, "What's Jimmy doing here?"

Einstein's voice Jimmy doesn't come to Mars, does he? He stays on earth and looks after his mother.

Jack's voice It should be Susan.

Jimmy's voice It says Jimmy here!

Einstein's voice It must be a mistake in the script.

Jimmy's voice Not another one. Look, why are we doing this rubbish? Why can't we do an Ayckbourn?

Einstein's voice Let's go back to my line, "Prepare for countdown," and then we'll just do the ten-nine-eight stuff.

Jack's voice Are you still recording, Joyce?

Joyce's voice Yes.

Einstein's voice We don't want any of this, dear. Can you cut it out of the tape afterwards?

Joyce's voice Cut what out?

Einstein's voice All of this.

Reverend Allsop's voice But not the next bit, Joyce. Don't cut the bit that goes ten-nine-eight . . .

Abrupt cut to sound of rocket taking off

Ultraviolet light snaps on

During the ensuing sequence the cast, in black costumes, gloves and masks, carry fluorescent-painted hardboard cut-outs of a rocket, flight of birds, clouds etc., which glow in the UV light

The rocket takes off. Music: "When You Wish Upon a Star". The rocket remains stationary. A flight of birds passes and disappears. Clouds pass and disappear. The Reverend Allsopp's presence is obvious from his glowing dog collar and white socks

A rainbow enters, collides with the rocket and both cut-outs fall to the floor. Muttering is heard about the darkness. The rainbow exits upside-down

The rocket reappears, angled as if in flight. The moon enters and, as it passes the rocket, the man in the moon's scowl turns to a smile. The moon exits. A comet enters, but the tail becomes detached from the nucleus, and it leaves the stage in two halves. A bar of Milky Way enters, crosses the stage and exits. The rocket disappears

Music: "I Only Have Eyes For You". As we hear "Are the stars out tonight?" stars appear then move in formation à la Busby Berkeley

The sound of a "Space Invaders" electronic game. Stars disappear. Space Invaders and spaceships enter and confront each other. The Invaders shoot the spaceships, each of which turns into a "splat". Full Lights snap on unexpectedly revealing players carrying props. Black-out, then UV light comes up again

The rocket enters. As the Invaders approach, a "Game over" card appears. The Invaders stop then disappear

Music: "When You Wish Upon A Star". "Game over" card turns into sign reading "Mars welcomes careful drivers"

Not realizing that it is fluorescent, Felicity casually carries the shark from one side of the stage to the other. The rocket lands. Music ends. Black-out

Everyone exits

In the Black-out, a Martian backdrop is flown in and an unknotted yellow balloon held out from the wings for Scene 2

SCENE 2

Mars

Atmospheric music

The Lights come up revealing Einstein, Reverend Allsopp and Susan moving over the Martian landscape in slow motion. The music ends

Einstein Well, everyone, we've just travelled two hundred million kilometres. What a giant spurt of Guildford spunk.

Susan I can't believe we've actually arrived on the angry, red planet, Professor.

The Lights suddenly change from open white to red

Einstein See for yourself, Susan. We're walking through Martian dust.

Susan Yes, isn't it awful? I wish I'd brought a can of Pledge.

Reverend Allsopp (*pointing at the balloon*) Look, Susan. Do you see that lustrous orb hovering remotely in the blackness of space?

Susan Yes, Daddy. What is it?

Reverend Allsopp The earth.

The balloon is accidentally released and propels itself round the stage

Einstein (*possibly holding up the deflated balloon*) It looks very different from out here, doesn't it?

Reverend Allsopp Enough of that daydreaming, Prof. We've got to find Roberta the Super-Townswoman.

Susan But where shall we look?

Everyone turns to the invisible Jack

Reverend Allsopp Why don't we . . . ?

Pause

Einstein No, Reverend, let Jack speak.

Silence

Hilda (*off*) Psst! Mrs Reece!

Einstein Hilda? Is that you?

Hilda (*off*) Yes, I'm all right now, Mrs Reece. I can carry on.

Einstein Was it the privet purée that did it? Oh, yes. I can see! You've got a little sparkle in your eyes and your hands have stopped doing that clawing movement. What a relief! Bravo, Hilda! Hilda's come up trumps, everyone.

Applause from Einstein and Reverend Allsopp

What a professional. Well, Jack! We anxiously await the inspired guidance that will lead us on the road to triumph.

Hilda (*off*) Yes. Well, I . . .

Pause. Then a clawing hand is briefly visible from the wings

(*Off*) I'm sorry, Mrs Reece. I don't think I . . . Oh, no! Oh, no!

Her voice recedes as we hear the sound of running feet and a slamming door

Einstein Could you manage just a couple of lines before you go, dear?

Susan Don't stop her, Phoebe! That suit's hired!

Einstein Oh, yes. Well . . . Jack's just gone to put some anti-freeze in the rocket. But fortunately we can maintain radio contact with him. (*He finds the powder compact; speaking into the lid*) This is Charlie Duracell Hedex calling Tango Foxtrot Hokey Cokey. Come in, Jack, and tell us where to look for my robot.

While waiting for reply he begins powdering his nose. Susan takes the powder compact out of his hands

Susan This is ... er ... Avon calling. What's that, Jack? Why, of course. How brilliant you are.

Reverend Allsopp Look! If these——

Susan Shut up. Go on, Jack. I'm listening. You think I'm the most beautiful girl in the world? I've never heard of such a thing.

Einstein I'm not surprised. Tell us about Jack's brainwave, dear.

Susan He says that, if we want to find the Martian hideout, we should look for a crater with empty milk bottles outside.

Reverend Allsopp (*looking in one direction*) Look! If these old eyes don't deceive me, there's a crater with Martian empties ... (*pointing in another direction*) ... over there.

Einstein Well spotted, Reverend. Let's go and investigate this mysterious crater while these youngsters keep watch.

Reverend Allsopp Remember, none of your canoodling, Susan and Jack.

Reverend Allsopp exits

Susan I'm cutting this next scene, Phoebe.

Einstein Thelma ... !

Susan Don't try and talk me out of it. Love scenes just do not work with less than two people.

Einstein But Monsieur Duvivier will be most upset.

Susan Well, he can do it then.

Einstein Is that your final word, Thelma?

Susan Yes.

Einstein All right. I'll tell the drama critic of the *Guild Monthly* to go home.

Susan What do you mean?

Einstein She's sitting in row D.

Einstein exits

After a moment's thought Susan turns her back on the audience and moves her hands up and down it to give the impression of a couple in a romantic clinch

Susan Jack, darling, I need you desperately. How I've longed for this moment when our lips would meet. Oh, Jack, Jack! I'm beside myself. (*One of her hands strays below her waist. Her other hand moves it up*) No, Jack. We mustn't. We're on Mars. (*The action is repeated*) Stop it, Jack. If you love me, you'll do the decent thing. Of course it's what I want. Oh, Jack! In that case—yes, yes, yes!

Reverend Allsopp and Einstein enter

Reverend Allsopp Susan, get a grip on yourself.

Susan It's all right, Daddy. I wasn't doing anything.

Reverend Allsopp The professor and I are just back from the crater with important news.

Susan Did you find the Martians?

Reverend Allsopp Calm down, Susan. Calm down, Jack. You know I can't understand you when you both speak at once. Now what did you say?
Susan Did you find the Martians?
Reverend Allsopp Yes.
Susan Hooray. And now we've got some important news for you.
Reverend Allsopp Well, out with it, my little one.
Susan Jack says that as I'm so attractive and charming he'd like to marry me. And he thinks I'm really intelligent as well. And a brilliant cellist.
Einstein You undersell yourself, dear.
Reverend Allsopp Bless my soul! Jack Braithwaite is to be my son-in-law, and we're hot on the trail of Roberta the Super-Townswoman. My, oh, my! What a wonderful day.

Music: "Zip-a-de-doo-dah." Colourful show lighting. Einstein, Susan and Reverend Allsopp go into an abysmally under-rehearsed production number, hindered further by the pauses that have to be left for specialities performed by the invisible Jack. "Martian" props are cackhandedly passed around while everyone tries to remember to mime to the voices on the record

Towards the end of the number, Indesit enters and joins in the routine

It finishes with Indesit pointing her ray-gun at the others (she holds the barrel and aims the handle). Full lighting comes up

Indesit I am a Martian. You are my prisoners.
Einstein (*referring to the gun*) Wrong way round, dear.
Indesit You are Martians. I am your prisoner.
Reverend Allsopp Take us to your leader.
Indesit No.
Reverend Allsopp Now see here, whatever your name is . . .
Indesit I am called Indesit, daughter of Listerine.
Reverend Allsopp How do you do. I am the Reverend Susan Einstein, this is Professor Indesit, and this is my fiancé, Jack Allsop, and his daughter, Thelma.
Einstein And I want the Super-Townswoman back.
Indesit Impossible. She is needed here on Mars.
Susan Give me one good reason.
Indesit Instead I will tell you the history of our planet. (*She moves* C)

> Long, long ago, when the planets were made,
> Mars was one of the best in the universe.
> Scones were cooked and bingo played,
> And we had more fun than the rest of the universe.
>
> Then all the men in the old Town Hall
> Said, "Let's take control of the universe.
> Mars is nice, but it's much too small;
> And we want the whole of the universe."
>
> Off went the rockets, dropping bombs on everything.
> Mars became the ruler of the Milky Way.

The men were glad, but the women were sad
Because the Guild activities became *passé*.

Oh, dear! No tombolas,
No keep fit to trim our girth,
No more fêtes, and no more jumble sales;
Then we got a telescope and looked at earth.

"Goodness me! See all the Tupperware!
"Goodness me!", we cried with glee.
"They make table mats out of raffia,
They've got home-made jam for tea."

Straight——

She is interrupted by Reverend Allsopp blowing his nose

Straight——

Reverend Allsopp blows his nose again. Indesit waits for him to finish

Reverend Allsopp (*thinking she's dried*) Straight away we want——
Indesit I know!

Straight away we wanted to regain these skills
And take our proper place in the universe.
Wars are the cause of Martian ills;
For fighting there's no space in the universe.

That's why we stole your Roberta.
She will make our lives serene.
She will bring us peace and pastry.
Hail Roberta as our queen!

Einstein (*to Allsopp*) And this line underneath your eye—you want to extend that like I've done, you see? Quite a bold statement required here ... You've done the poem, have you, dear? Sorry, I was on another planet. No, Jack, leave this to me. Don't think we're not sympathetic, Indesit, because life without a Braun Multipractic Blender must be intolerable. But stealing other people's robots is not the answer.
Indesit (*turning her back*) We are desperate women.
Reverend Allsopp No, Jack! Don't be a fool!

Reverend Allsopp, Einstein and Susan watch the invisible Jack as he supposedly creeps up behind Indesit in an attempt to grab her gun. Indesit struggles with nobody. At one point Jack seems to be gaining the upper hand, and the gun is pointed at Indesit's head. But with a supreme effort Indesit forces the gun away and fires it into thin air

Susan Jack, darling!
Reverend Allsopp Oh, no. Neutralized again.
Indesit You leave me no alternative. You will be taken to the dungeons, where you will be castrated.

Everyone winces with embarrassment

What's the matter?
Susan The word is incarcerated.
Indesit What did I say?
Susan Oh, get on with it, do!
Indesit Quick business and no funny marching.

Indesit marches off R, *thinking the others are following. But they have marched off* L

A pause

Susan, Einstein and Reverend Allsopp enter L *and follow Indesit off* R

Black-out

Indesit, Einstein, Susan and Reverend Allsopp enter DR

The Lights come up on a jail DR. *Indesit is seated on a chair above the bars. She has keys and a beer bottle. Einstein, Reverend Allsopp and Susan are huddled below the bars*

Let that be a lesson to you, my fine earthlings. (*After a quick consultation, she changes places with the others*) Let that be a lesson to you, my fine earthlings. (*She drinks*) You can cool your heels in there until tomorrow morning when you'll be tried as spies. (*She drinks*) Hmmm. This Martian beer is making me quite sleepy. (*She sleeps, but while "asleep" slowly places the bottle on the floor*)
Reverend Allsopp What a pickle. We've got to break out of this dungeon and find somewhere to get a decent cup of tea.
Susan And I want to wash my hair.
Reverend Allsopp Any ideas, Jack?
Susan No good asking Jack, Daddy. He's still poorly after that last bout of neutralization.
Einstein Yes, he's not really with us, is he? What I suggest is that we steal Indesit's keys. She'll never notice while she's in that drunken sleep.
Susan Can you reach them?
Einstein Yes, easily. (*After a pause*) You're too far away. Felicity!
Indesit What?
Einstein Come a bit nearer.

Indesit moves her chair a fraction closer to the bars

That's not much help, is it?
Indesit I'm not moving again. It's silly.
Einstein Oh, sorry if it's not *real* enough, Meryl Streep. Gordon, would you mind?

Einstein and Reverend Allsopp move the bars next to Indesit

It was the biggest mistake of my life lending her my copy of *Amateur Stage*. Now she thinks she knows everything.
Susan That's it, Professor. Gently pull the keys through the bars.

Einstein I can do without the instructions, thank you. I'm perfectly capable . . .

He breaks off as he realizes his bracelets are preventing him from reaching through the bars. After ineffectual wiggling, he withdraws his arm, calmly walks round the bars and begins tugging at Indesit's keys. They are attached to her belt and Einstein cannot free them. There is a huge struggle with Indesit being heaved this way and that as Einstein becomes more desperate. Finally they both fall to the floor

Indesit That's my poorly leg!
Susan (*flatly*) Careful you don't wake her, Professor.
Einstein Hurrah! The keys are mine!

Black-out

> *Indesit and Reverend Allsopp exit taking the chair and bars*

> *Einstein and Susan are discovered as the Lights come up*

Susan Professor, we've turned this crater upside down and we still haven't found Roberta.
Einstein We must keep searching.
Susan But we've turned this crater upside down and we still haven't found her.

Pause

Einstein There's no need to cry, Susan.

Taken aback, Susan begins crying

So come on, back on your feet.

Susan sinks to the floor and then rises again

Susan I can't go on any more. I want to go home. The foxgloves will be in bloom and Mummy will be restoring last summer's sling-backs with Lady Esquire.
Einstein There, there. Take my hanky. (*He pulls out a handkerchief and with it about a pound's worth of loose change, which cascades on to the floor*)
Susan Listen!
Einstein It sounds as if Roberta's teaching the Martians how to do the Hoovering.

Sound of a doorbell

Susan And here comes Roberta now, bounding towards us like a new-born gazelle.

> *Preceded by groans and straining, Reverend Allsopp and Indesit enter with the unconscious Roberta slung between their shoulders*

Einstein I know you're pleased to see us, Roberta, but this is ridiculous.
Susan Put me down, Roberta.
Einstein Speed is of the essence, my girl. Lead us to the rocket.
Indesit Hold it right there, earthling fools.

Einstein
Reverend Allsopp } (*together*) Indesit!
Susan

Indesit throws Roberta on to Allsopp

Indesit Take her.
Reverend Allsopp I can't.
Indesit I've got to get round the other side. Nobody move!

Indesit exits L

Einstein Indesit!
Indesit (*off*) Won't be a sec.
Einstein We're waiting for you to catch us unexpectedly, dear.

Indesit enters R

Indesit Sorry about that. I fell in a Martian canal.
Einstein We won't bother with the ad libbing, Felicity.
Indesit Oh. So you thought you could outwit me, did you?
Susan Look, Indesit, let's discuss this calmly over a cup of tea. Tea, everyone?
Einstein Half a cup for me.
Reverend Allsopp Two sweeteners, please.
Susan Roberta?
Einstein She'll have a can of Three-in-One.
Indesit Reach for the sky, all of you.

Einstein and Susan do so

(*To Reverend Allsopp*) Reach for the sky.

Reverend Allsopp somehow manages to half-raise his arms while supporting Roberta

You have tried my patience to the utmost. You will suffer the supreme punishment.
Susan What could be worse than this?

Reverend Allsopp drops Roberta

Roberta dozily crawls off

Indesit You will be executed immediately.
Mrs Reece (*to the audience*) Well, while I remember, let's have the results of the Flower Arranging Competition.

Susan and Reverend Allsopp exit. Gordon enters with a table bearing two unsightly flower arrangements

Mrs Reece As you know it was a very keenly fought contest this year. But we've managed to whittle the entrants down to just two finalists, and here they are. The theme was "Out of This World". And who would deny that these creations are like nothing on earth? The runner-up will receive a pair

of non-slip gardening gloves and a Boots record token. And the winner
will receive a ... rusty bird table?

Gordon Rustic.

Mrs Reece Oh, yes. A rustic bird table. And a set of willow pattern coasters.
So now, to make the final decision, we're very pleased to welcome the
gardening correspondent of the *Guild Monthly*, Mrs [*whoever*].

Mrs Reece encourages applause and the audience member mounts the stage

Well, thank you for coming here tonight and, without further ado, I'll let
you choose this year's runner-up. Off you go. Who's going to be the
recipient of the non-slip gardening gloves?

The audience member chooses an arrangement

That one? Will you pass me the display, please, Gordon? Thank you.
Well, this is called "Blossoms on Uranus" and it's the work of Mrs Hilda
Bristow. (*Into the wings*) Is she out of the to—— can she get off the ... ?
She can't. Well, never mind. Just knock at the door and tell her she's won
the gardening gloves she donated.

*To the agitation of Gordon, Norah crawls back on stage and collapses again
by the table*

(*To the audience*) So we're agreed then, are we, Mrs [*whoever*], on this
year's first prizewinner? Splendid. Gordon! Don't drift off, dear. Give me
this thing, will you? Thank you. This beautiful flower arrangement is
called "Beautiful Flower Arrangement" and it's by Felicity Cheshire. Is
she there?

Felicity pokes her head in

Felicity Have I won?

Mrs Reece Yes, dear. The bird table.

Felicity Oh, how wonderful! Thank you, Mrs [*whoever*].

Mrs Reece Would you take this, please, Gordon, and be careful with it.

The winning flower arrangement falls to pieces in Gordon's hands

I told you to be careful!

Felicity begins crying

Felicity, he didn't do it on purpose. Did you? No. Come on, dear. It's
your own fault. You should have used more Uhu. Gordon, would you
mind ... ?

*Gordon ushers Felicity into the wings. He then takes hold of Norah's feet
and begins dragging her off. She is holding on to the table legs and pulls the
table off with her*

Norah (*to the audience member*) Hello, darling! Look, there's a table
following me.

Mrs Reece (*to the audience member*) Take no notice. Thank you very much
for coming along and giving us the benefit of your wisdom. And don't go

away just yet because we've got a little surprise for you. It's a rather special day for you today, isn't it? Yes, it is! Don't be bashful. We know all about it. So we're going to give you something we've been preparing all evening. Joyce! You know what to do.

The National Anthem is heard

No, dear. The lights.

The Lights dim to half

All right, folk. In you all come.

Gordon, Thelma and Felicity enter with a birthday cake decorated with lit candles

Everyone sings "Happy Birthday". The Lights return to full

Make a wish!

The audience member attempts to blow out trick candles, which re-light

More puff, dear. Try again. Let me try. No, we don't want everybody trying. Don't be ridiculous. Take them away, Gordon. Dowse them in something. (*She presents the audience member with the cake*) Bon appétit!

Gordon removes the candles. The audience member returns to her seat. Gordon, Felicity and Thelma resume their places for the play

Well, we'll be going back to Mars in a moment. But just before we do, I'd like to remind those who are coming to the handicraft class this Thursday that we'll be making the bridesmaids' head-dresses for Sandra Rathbone's forthcoming nuptials. I don't know about you, but I'm getting all misty-eyed just thinking about it. But that's enough of that.

Indesit You will all be executed immediately.

Mrs Reece Mrs Rathbone's given me the patterns. She wants white pillboxes with detached scallops in baby pink, which will look absolutely gorgeous.

Indesit You will all be executed ...

Mrs Reece So, anyway, what I was going to say is that, if you're coming, can you bring a ball of Coats Chain Mercer Number Twenty and a needle?

Thelma Can I make a suggestion?

Mrs Reece Why not, Thelma? It's a communal effort.

Thelma Can we get back to the play?

Mrs Reece Oh. Sorry.

Indesit You will all be executed immediately.

Susan Wait a minute, Indesit. You said that Martian women wanted peace. Surely you don't really want to kill us?

Indesit Not really, no.

Susan Good because I've got a much better idea. We can share Roberta. You can have her for half the year, and we can have her for the other half.

Indesit I think it would be better if we had her on alternate months except for June, when we'd only want her at weekends and on early closing days.

Reverend Allsopp Well, we'd definitely want her for Lent, All Saints and the Harvest Festival. You can have her for months without an R in them.
Einstein What do you think, Jack?

Silence

I think that's the best idea yet.
Indesit I agree.
Susan That's settled then. Now! Let's have that cup of tea!

Black-out during which there is much scraping and complaining as a table and three chairs are set

Reverend Allsopp exits

The Lights come up revealing a table covered with a chequered cloth and set for tea: cups and saucers, teapot, milk jug, sugar, napkins, plate of (foam-rubber) sandwiches and large cream cake. Roberta is slumped in a chair above the table, Susan is to her L and Indesit to her R. Einstein is trying to prop Roberta upright. As a last resort he ducks down behind Roberta and puts his arms underneath Roberta's armpits. He then moves his own hands about on the table to give the impression that Roberta is more alert than she is

Indesit Won't the men be joining us, Susan?
Susan No, they're still tinkering about with the rocket. I think there's a bit of trouble with those things that slow you down when you reach the earth's atmosphere.
Indesit Are they the sticky-out things with the wires on them?
Susan I wouldn't know. It means nothing to me.
Indesit Nor me. I'd rather have a bit of a natter.
Susan Yes. You know I sometimes think there's more of a gulf between men and women than there is between Mars and earth.
Indesit Especially now we're such friends. Shall I be mother?
Susan Why don't we let Roberta do the honours? She is programmed to be the perfect hostess.
Indesit (*uncertainly*) Very well.
Susan You may serve tea, Roberta.

Einstein gives the thumbs-up sign. His hands then begin feeling about the table for the teapot. Susan assists him

She's really marvellous around the house. I don't know what we'd do without her.
Indesit I'm sure.

Einstein pours tea willy-nilly. Susan and Indesit move the cups around trying to catch some of it

Susan Milk?
Indesit Just a drop.

Susan puts the milk in Einstein's hand, then quickly places a cup underneath it. The jug remains poised and nothing happens

Thank you.

Abruptly Einstein moves the jug elsewhere and pours milk on the table

No, on second thoughts I'll have it black.
Susan So will I. You don't take sugar, do you?
Indesit No!
Susan No, nor do I.

Einstein's hands fumble for the sugar

We don't want sugar, thank you, Roberta.

Einstein finds the sugar

Forget about the sugar, thank you! (*She wrenches the bowl from Einstein's hand*) I still have a few surplus pounds to get rid of.
Indesit Me, too.

Roberta is nonplussed by Einstein's hand scratching her nose

Susan (*drinking*) Oh, that's better.
Indesit (*drinking*) Tea is such a comfort, isn't it?

Einstein picks up a cup and places it at Roberta's lips. She turns her head away and he pours the tea over her shoulder

Susan Cucumber sandwich?
Indesit Love one.

Einstein's hands feel about, splattering into the cream cake

Susan That's the cake, Roberta. (*To Indesit*) I often confuse cucumber sandwiches with cake, don't you?
Indesit Yes, they are very similar.

Einstein's hand locates the sandwiches, then pokes and squeezes them to make sure what they are

Susan Did you know Roberta can butter fifty sandwiches and whip up a chocolate torte simultaneously?
Indesit (*disbelievingly*) Really?

Einstein tips the sandwiches into Indesit's lap

Susan It's hard to credit, I'll grant you that.

Indesit retrieves the sandwiches

What a lovely day, isn't it?
Indesit All the lovelier because our planets are united.
Susan I'll drink to that.

Einstein finds the teapot and pours tea on the table. Susan takes it out of his hand. Indesit picks up a sodden sandwich and looks distastefully at the tea dripping out of it. She carefully squeezes it out

Indesit What delicious sandwiches. (*She appears to put it in her mouth, but palms it at the last moment, chews vigorously, and then flings the sandwich over her shoulder*) Scrumptious.
Susan Would you like another?
Indesit No, no, no!

She prevents Einstein from picking up the sandwich plate again

Thank you all the same.

Instead Einstein tries to push a sandwich into Roberta's mouth. The sandwich is prodded into Roberta's forehead and both cheeks. Perplexed, Roberta brings her own hands out and takes hold of Einstein's right hand. Einstein's left hand scratches Roberta's temple. While Roberta blearily follows the action, Einstein's left hand peels Roberta's left hand off his right, then, her right hand off his right. Both pairs of hands are now visible. Roberta studies them, silently trying to comprehend why she has four hands. Einstein's hands then put Roberta's out of the way. His own reappear through Roberta's armpits and he finds the cream cake, lifting it up and moving it around threateningly

Susan Well! What else can I tempt you with?
Indesit I'm as full as an egg.
Susan Yes, I don't think I could manage anything else either. So don't do anything you may regret, Roberta.
Roberta What's happening? (*Her eyes dazedly follow the progress of the cake*) What's that? Is that for me?
Susan We sincerely hope so.
Roberta I couldn't possibly.

Einstein's hands slowly replace the cake on the table. Susan and Indesit relax

Susan Well, we must do this more often.
Indesit Yes, it's been delight——

Roberta tips forward, head first into the cake

Delightful.

Reverend Allsopp enters, laughing

Reverend Allsopp Ha-ha-ha-ha-ha. You certainly can tell them, Jack. Ha-ha-ha-ha-ha.
Susan Daddy! Jack! Professor!

Einstein rises

Einstein Sorry. I just dropped my ear-ring.
Susan Your what?
Einstein (*gruffly*) I mean my cuff-link.
Reverend Allsopp Good news, girls: the rocket is ready for our return to earth.
Susan Then we must take our leave. Professor, I expect you'll want to collect some samples before we go.
Einstein I'm not coming with you, Susan.

Susan You mean ... ?

Einstein That's right, Susan. Mars and earth have so much valuable information to exchange. I can learn to cross the frontier of time itself, and the Martians want to know all about smocking, collage, tapestry and rug-making.

Indesit We would be greatly honoured, Professor, if you and Roberta would consent to rule Mars as king and queen.

Reverend Allsopp (*too early*) Hurrah.

Einstein Gladly.

Susan
Indesit } (*together*) Hurrah!
Reverend Allsopp

Roberta That always happens with nylon.

Embarrassed hiatus

Indesit Good. I will make immediate preparations for the coronation.

Indesit exits

Susan You will come back to earth for the wedding, won't you, professor?

Einstein What wedding's that, Susan?

Susan Why, my wedding to Jack, you silly old scientist!

Einstein I was only joking, Susan. Of course I'll be there.

Einstein
Susan } (*together*) Ha-ha-ha-ha-ha!

Reverend Allsopp (*too late*) Ha-ha.

Susan Everything has——

Roberta (*hysterical*) Ha-ha-ha-ha-ha-ha!

Einstein puts his hand over her mouth

Susan Everything has worked out so wonderfully. Jack is going to be as rich as Croesus by selling this story to the papers, I'm going to be his wife, and we're going to have the dearest little cottage with roses round the door and an old donkey peeping over the picket fence. Also I've been the first woman on Mars. Yes, I am crying, Jack, but they're tears of happiness.

Roberta too bursts into tears and is silenced again

Reverend Allsopp Let's get ready, everyone. Here comes Indesit with the professor's crown.

Fanfare. Einstein is seated

Indesit enters, bearing a crown

Indesit (*holding it over Einstein's head*) By the power vested in me, I hereby crown you King of Mars.

She goes to place the crown on his head, but it is so large that it drops straight down on to his shoulders. Everybody cheers and waves. Reverend Allsopp waves Roberta's hand. Tableau

Einstein (*into the wings*) Lights!

Black-out. Music

The company take their calls. If another female is available, she could come on last, in trenchcoat and trilby hat with a press card in the band, as the hitherto unseen Hilda

CURTAIN

FURNITURE AND PROPERTY LIST

PROLOGUE

On stage: Nil

Off stage: Table, curtain A **(Gordon** and **Thelma)**
Ironing board, curtain B **(Norah)**
Vacuum cleaner, curtain C **(Felicity)**
Fluorescent-painted hardboard shark cut-out **(Felicity)**
Bucket, curtain D **(Thelma)**
Plastic sack marked "Gordon's make-up" **(Norah)**
Table or desk with drawer **(Felicity)**
4 chairs **(Felicity)**
Iron **(Felicity)**
Numerous bric-à-brac, including portrait of "The Laughing Cavalier"
    Gordon's notes, wind-up toy, handbag containing a jar of capsules
    (Felicity)

Personal: **Mrs Reece:** programmes, bracelets, handbag

ACT I

On stage: All items from Prologue

Off stage: Broom **(Stage management)**
Electric torch **(Gordon)**
Box of matches **(Gordon)**
Test tube **(Professor Einstein)**
Jar of capsules **(Mrs Allsopp)**
Semaphore flags **(Jimmy)**

Personal: **Mrs Tompkins:** duster
Indesit: walkie-talkie with detachable aerial, ray-gun in holster (worn
    throughout)
Professor Einstein: pen-torch, bracelets (worn throughout)
Susan: towel

ENTR'ACTE

Strike: All items

Off stage: Small photos **(Stage management)**

Personal: **Mrs Reece:** handbag

ACT II
SCENE 1

On stage: Nil

Off stage: Fluorescent-painted hardboard cut-outs of a rocket, flight of birds, clouds, rainbow, moon, comet, bar of Milky Way, stars, Space Invaders with "Splat" sign on reverse, spaceships, "Game Over"/ "Mars welcomes careful drivers" card **(Company)**

SCENE 2

On stage: "Martian" props

Off stage: Unknotted yellow balloon **(Stage management)**
                Jail bars **(Susan, Einstein, Reverend Allsopp)**
                Chair, bottle of beer **(Indesit)**
                Table. *On it*: 2 unsightly flower arrangements **(Gordon)**
                Birthday cake decorated with trick lighted candles **(Gordon, Thelma
                and Felicity)**

During Black out on page 36

Set: Table covered with chequered cloth. *On it*: 3 cups and saucers, teapot containing tea, milk jug with milk, sugar, napkins, plate of (foam-rubber) sandwiches, large cream cake
                3 chairs

Off stage: Crown **(Indesit)**

Personal: **Einstein:** powder compact, handkerchief, £1 in loose change
                Reverend Allsopp: handkerchief
                Indesit: keys

LIGHTING PLOT

Property fittings required: nil
Various simple settings

PROLOGUE

To open: Stage and house lights on

Cue 1   **Felicity** exits   (Page 3)
             Fade to Black-out

ACT I

To open: Full general lighting

Cue 2   **Einstein:** "... see you in outer space."   (Page 22)
             Black-out, when ready bring up house lights

ENTR'ACTE

To open: House lights on, spot c

Cue 3   **Mrs Reece:** "... the snaps we took in London?"   (Page 23)
             Snap off spot

Cue 4   **Mrs Reece:** "I want to assure you all ..."   (Page 23)
             Snap on and off variety of lights in sequence

Cue 5   **Mrs Reece:** "Underneath the baking soda."   (Page 23)
             Spot c

Cue 6   **Mrs Reece** hustles **Thelma** off   (Page 24)
             Fade to Black-out

ACT II, Scene 1

To open: Black-out

Cue 7   Sound effect of rocket taking off   (Page 25)
             Snap on UV light

Cue 8   "Splat" sign appears   (Page 26)
             *Snap on full general lighting; pause; black-out, then return
             to UV lighting*

Cue 9   Music ends   (Page 26)
             Black-out

ACT II, SCENE 2

To open:	General lighting	
Cue 10	**Susan:** ". . . angry, red planet, Professor." *Change to red lighting*	(Page 26)
Cue 11	**Reverend Allsopp:** "What a wonderful day." *Change to colourful show lighting*	(Page 29)
Cue 12	**Indesit** points her ray-gun at the others *Change to full general lighting*	(Page 29)
Cue 13	**Susan, Einstein** and **Reverend Allsopp** follow **Indesit** off R *Black-out; when ready bring up lighting* DR	(Page 31)
Cue 14	**Einstein:** "Hurrah! The keys are mine!" *Black-out; when ready bring up full general lighting*	(Page 32)
Cue 15	**Mrs Reece:** "No, dear. The lights." *Dim to half*	(Page 35)
Cue 16	After everyone has sung "Happy Birthday" *Return to full lighting*	(Page 35)
Cue 17	**Susan:** ". . . that cup of tea!" *Black-out; when ready bring up full general lighting*	(Page 36)
Cue 18	**Einstein:** "Lights!" *Black-out; when ready bring up full general lighting*	(Page 40)

EFFECTS PLOT

PROLOGUE

ACT I

ACT II